Library Technology
REPORTS
Expert Guides to Library Systems and Services

Understanding the Semantic Web: Bibliographic Data and Metadata

Karen Coyle

ALA TechSource
www.alatechsource.org

Library Technology
R E P O R T S

American Library Association

50 East Huron St.
Chicago, IL 60611-2795 USA
www.alatechsource.org
800-545-2433, ext. 4299
312-944-6780
312-280-5275 (fax)

Advertising Representative

Brian Searles, Ad Sales Manager
ALA Publishing Dept.
bsearles@ala.org
312-280-5282
1-800-545-2433, ext. 5282

ALA TechSource Editor

Dan Freeman
dfreeman@ala.org
312-280-5413

Copy Editor

Judith Lauber

Administrative Assistant

Judy Foley
jfoley@ala.org
800-545-2433, ext. 4272
312-280-5275 (fax)

Production and Design

ALA Production Services: Troy D. Linker
and Karen Sheets de Gracia

Library Technology Reports (ISSN 0024-2586) is published eight times a year (January, March, April, June, July, September, October, and December) by American Library Association, 50 E. Huron St., Chicago, IL 60611. It is managed by ALA TechSource, a unit of the publishing department of ALA. Periodical postage paid at Chicago, Illinois, and at additional mailing offices. POSTMASTER: Send address changes to Library Technology Reports, 50 E. Huron St., Chicago, IL 60611.

ALA TechSource
www.alatechsource.org

About the Author

Karen Coyle is a librarian and a consultant in the area of digital libraries. She worked for over 20 years at the University of California in the California Digital Library, has served on library and information standards committees, and had written frequently on technical topics ranging from metadata development, technology management and system design, and on policy area such as copyright and privacy.

Abstract

The rise of a new information environment—the World Wide Web—has revealed the downside of the long history that libraries have with metadata. The question that we must face, and that we must face sooner rather than later, is how we can best transform our data so that it can become part of the dominant information environment that is the Web. This issue of "Library Technology Reports" examines how this transformation can occur, and what can be done to help facilitate it.

The movement of library data into the linked data cloud is not as far off as it might seem. Like the scientific databases, the metadata already exists and is in a data format. Some transformation of the data to a format compatible with the semantic Web will be necessary, but the encoding that has already been done (mainly in the MARC format) and the degree of vocabulary control that exists facilitate the transformation. It truly is a matter of transformation, at least in a first step. After that, the only limits are those of the imagination of information seekers all over the globe.

Subscriptions

For more information about subscriptions and individual issues for purchase, call the ALA Customer Service Center at 1-800-545-2433 and press 5 for assistance, or visit www.alatechsource.org.

Table of Contents

Chapter 1

Library Data in a Modern Context

Abstract

This chapter of "Understanding the Semantic Web: Bibliographic Data and Metadata" explores the history of library data and where it stands in a modern context. The rise of a new information environment—the World Wide Web—has revealed the downside of the long history that libraries have with metadata. The question that we must face, and that we must face sooner rather than later, is how we can best transform our data so that it can become part of the dominant information environment that is the Web.

The larger the library is, the more you must distinguish the books from each other, and consequently the more fully and more accurately you must catalogue them. . . When I come to a great and national library, where I have the editions or works of "Abelard," I have a right to find those editions and works so well distinguished from each other that I may get exactly the particular one which I want.

—Sir Anthony Panizzi[1]

We can trace the origins of modern library cataloging practice back to the 1830s and Anthony Panizzi's 91 rules. Panizzi's singular insight was that a large catalog needed consistency in its entries if it was to serve the user. The years that followed brought waves of change that transformed the world socially, technologically, and intellectually. These changes were matched by a related evolution of libraries and library catalogs. The card catalog came about at the time of the industrial revolution, which was marked by a great increase in the production of printed materials. The true mechanization of the catalog was not possible until much more recent times, when advanced computer technology allowed the creation of the Online Public Access Catalog (OPAC) in the 1980s. Some might say that the term *OPAC* already sounds quaint to the ears of twenty-first-century librarians.

With each era, conceptual changes to the catalog have come in response to related changes in the catalog's context. Some changes in cataloging rules have addressed the new types of material that libraries must catalog, for instance, the changes that came with the emergence of recorded sound and films. Changes in the workflow of cataloging have been necessary to respond to the increased production of information resources. Technology itself has offered opportunities for change.

If there is one constant, it is that throughout these nearly two centuries, the modern library has continually transformed itself in an effort to respond to the needs of its contemporary user.

Today, we face another significant time of change that is being prompted by today's library user. This user no longer visits the physical library as his primary source of information, but seeks and creates information while connected to the global computer network. The change that libraries will need to make in response must include the transformation of the library's public catalog from a stand-alone database of bibliographic records to a highly hyperlinked data set that can interact with information resources on the World Wide Web. The library data can then be integrated into the virtual working spaces of the users served by the library.

If all of this sounds otherworldly and vague, it is because there is no specific vision of where these changes will lead us. The crystal ball is unfortunately shortsighted, in no small part because this is a time of rapid change in many aspects of the information ecology. The few things that are certain, however, point to the Web, and its eventual successors, as the place to be. For libraries, this means yet another evolutionary step in the library of our catalog: from metadata to meta<u>DATA</u>.

Defining Metadata

The most common definition of *metadata* is "data about data." This short, catchy definition is worthy of a successful advertising campaign. Unfortunately, it doesn't really help us understand metadata, and is actually somewhat incorrect. A more useful definition is decidedly less snappy, but can help us understand the helpful role that metadata can play in facilitating information access. In fact, a functional definition gives us a viable roadmap for our own studies of metadata utility and quality.

So here it goes—metadata is constructed, constructive, and actionable:

- **Constructed:** Metadata is not found in nature. It is entirely an invention; it is an artificiality.

- **Constructive:** Metadata is constructed for some purpose, some activity, to solve some problem. The proliferation of metadata formats that seem similar on the surface is often evidence of different definitions of needs or of different contexts. We may dream of a universal set of metadata for some set of things, like biological entities, printed books, or a calendar of events, but are likely to be disappointed in practice.

- **Actionable:** The point of metadata is to be useful in some way. This means that it is important that one can act on the metadata in a way that satisfies some needs.

Figure 1
Map of the earth with no Metadata.

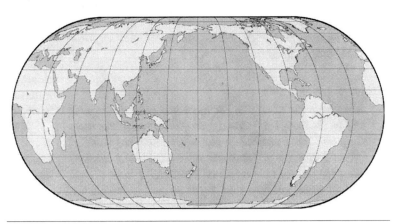

Figure 2
Map of the earth with Metadata—latitude and longitude.

From this rather lengthy definition, it is undoubtedly evident that the creation of good, functional metadata depends greatly on an understanding of the potential uses of the metadata and of the needs that the metadata must be designed to satisfy. It's not uncommon for people to approach the creation of metadata as a philosophical activity, attempting to define some kind of perfect universe for the things to be described. Metadata developed on theoretical, religious, or philosophical principles may be intellectually pleasing, but is unlikely to get the job done. Instead, the metadata that we find ourselves using every day is the metadata that we can use to accomplish some task. For example, figure 1 shows the earth.

Figure 2 is how we see the earth with the metadata of longitude and latitude.

The use of longitude and latitude is so familiar to us that it's almost easy to forget that the earth does not really have lines running along its axes. There are no lines

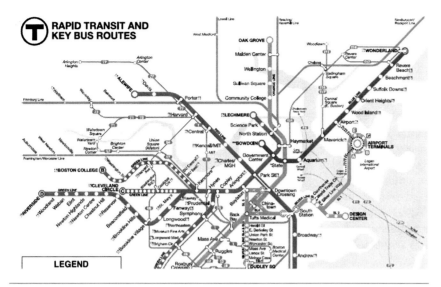

Figure 3
Boston subway map.

Team Batting	More Stats	Glossary · Click headers to sort · SHARE · CSV · PRE · LINK · ☑ Hide non-qualifiers for rate st

Rk	Pos		Age	G	PA	AB	R	H	2B	3B	HR	RBI	SB	CS	BB	SO	BA	OBP	SLG	OPS	OPS+	TB	GDP	HBP	SH	SF	IBB
1	C	Jorge Posada#	37	111	438	383	55	109	25	0	22	81	1	0	48	101	.285	.363	.522	.885	130	200	13	2	0	5	4
2	1B	Mark Teixeira#	29	156	707	609	103	178	43	3	39	122	2	0	81	114	.292	.383	.565	.948	146	344	13	12	0	5	9
3	2B	Robinson Cano*	26	161	674	637	103	204	48	2	25	85	5	7	30	63	.320	.352	.520	.871	126	331	22	3	0	4	2
4	SS	Derek Jeter	35	153	716	634	107	212	27	1	18	66	30	5	72	90	.334	.406	.465	.871	129	295	18	5	4	1	4
5	3B	Alex Rodriguez	33	124	535	444	78	127	17	1	30	100	14	2	80	97	.286	.402	.532	.933	143	236	13	8	0	3	7
6	LF	Johnny Damon*	35	143	626	550	107	155	36	3	24	82	12	0	71	98	.282	.365	.489	.854	123	269	9	2	2	1	1
7	CF	Melky Cabrera#	24	154	540	485	66	133	28	1	13	68	10	2	43	59	.274	.336	.416	.752	97	202	15	4	4	4	4
8	RF	Nick Swisher#	28	150	607	498	84	124	35	1	29	82	0	0	97	126	.249	.371	.498	.869	126	248	13	3	3	6	2
9	DH	Hideki Matsui*	35	142	526	456	62	125	21	1	28	90	0	1	64	75	.274	.367	.509	.876	128	232	4	4	0	2	1
Rk	Pos		Age	G	PA	AB	R	H	2B	3B	HR	RBI	SB	CS	BB	SO	BA	OBP	SLG	OPS	OPS+	TB	GDP	HBP	SH	SF	IBB
10	CF	Brett Gardner*	25	108	284	248	48	67	6	6	3	23	26	5	26	40	.270	.345	.379	.724	91	94	3	3	6	1	0
11	C	Jose Molina	34	52	155	138	15	30	4	0	1	11	0	0	14	28	.217	.292	.268	.560	49	37	6	1	1	1	0
12	IF	Ramiro Pena#	23	69	121	115	17	33	6	1	1	10	4	1	5	20	.287	.317	.383	.699	83	44	2	0	1	0	0
13	C	Francisco Cervelli	23	42	101	94	13	28	4	0	1	11	0	3	2	11	.298	.309	.372	.682	79	35	1	0	4	1	0
14	RF	Eric Hinske*	31	39	98	84	13	19	3	0	7	14	1	0	10	25	.226	.316	.512	.828	113	43	2	2	0	2	1
15	UT	Jerry Hairston	33	45	93	76	15	18	5	0	2	12	0	1	11	8	.237	.352	.382	.733	94	29	1	3	2	1	0
16	3B	Cody Ransom	33	31	86	79	11	15	9	1	0	10	2	0	7	25	.190	.256	.329	.585	53	26	3	0	0	0	0
17	UT	Xavier Nady	30	7	29	28	4	8	4	0	0	2	0	0	1	6	.286	.310	.429	.739	92	12	2	0	0	0	0
18	C	Kevin Cash	31	10	28	26	1	6	2	0	0	3	0	0	0	5	.231	.250	.308	.558	46	8	1	1	0	1	0
19	3B	Angel Berroa	31	21	24	22	6	3	1	0	0	1	0	0	0	6	.136	.174	.182	.356	-6	4	1	1	1	0	0
20	UT	Shelley Duncan	29	11	15	15	1	3	0	0	0	1	0	0	0	5	.200	.200	.200	.400	6	3	0	0	0	0	0

Figure 4
Baseball as metadata [source: www.baseball-reference.com].

Figure 3 is a typical subway map. If you were to superimpose this map over the city it represents, you'd find that the subway map isn't "true," in the sense that it is neither to scale nor are the stations located where they would be on a map based on longitude and latitude. This, however, isn't a defect of the subway map, because that isn't the purpose or function of the map. The map is intended to help us navigate the subway lines, often underground. We need to know where to change from one line to another, and in which direction to take the train. These maps leave out a great number of details that a geographer would consider essential in a map of the area. And yet they perform their job incredibly well, to the point that one can arrive in a city for the first time, perhaps even with only a limited understanding of the local language, and find one's way. These maps are a good example of functionality in metadata.

Metadata can also serve the function of substituting for something we cannot otherwise work with. The examples in figure 4 and 5—baseball statistics and a visualization of human DNA (Figure 5 on next page)— show how metadata can represent an otherwise intangible thing or concept. In the case of the baseball statistics, this metadata makes it possible to characterize a game, a player, or even an entire season and to make comparisons from one such representation to another. If you've ever spent time with enthusiasts of the game, you know that this seemingly abstract reduction of the game to fractions and percentages can be every bit as real to those fans as the very game itself. This metadata, as opposed to the experience of the game itself, provides concrete measurements that can answer burning questions like who the best player on the team might be. As for the DNA example, although we can be sure that our genetic material is not composed of differently shaded ovals, the microscopic size of the genome makes any communication about it impossible without a contrived representation.

marking points on the earth. Longitude and latitude were invented because these measurements were essential for the navigation of a vast ocean that provided no visual points of reference that humans could use. Longitude and latitude are a good example of constructed and constructive data. This metadata is also actionable; initially you had to have a clear sky and a sextant. Today we are fortunate to have sophisticated global positioning systems to tell us, with considerable accuracy, where on the planet we are currently located, yet these systems still use the planetary metadata that was developed over two thousand years ago.

There are other navigation systems, however, that aren't based on longitude and latitude. As a matter of fact, in terms of earthly location they are fairly inaccurate. Yet, they serve their users.

MetaDATA

While longitude and latitude were useful even in ancient times, today's metadata must be in a form that can be processed by computers, and the sense that it is "actionable" really needs to be interpreted as being "actionable by electronic machines." Even when the final goal is to display the data to humans in an understandable form, the data will undergo some machine processing on the way to its destination on a screen on in printed form. This need to be manipulated by a computer puts constraints on how the metadata is constructed. Machine-actionable metadata, however, provides possibilities that cannot be achieved with pre–computer era metadata that was designed to be read and interpreted by humans. Take a look at the two maps in figures 6 and 7.

Although they cover the same area and have approximately the same features, the functionality a user can get from them differs greatly. The map in figure 6 is a printed road map. I can use it to find my way from one city to another by reading the map image. Beyond that, though, this map is essentially inert. The map in figure 7 looks much like the map in figure 6, but what we see here is only one possible display. The map in figure 7 has machine-actionable metadata behind it. That allows the addition of features and gives users the ability to reuse it in ways that cannot be done with the paper map. The paper map always looks the same, with the same information. The machine-actionable map, however, can be used to create any number of different images, such to display all of the hotels in the downtown area (see figure 8) or to show bicycle paths or walking tours. These features can be presented because they all make use of the underlying layers of metadata.

The details that make this map so useful are generally hidden from human users. Figure 9 is an example of those details from an open source map service.

Not only can we create different displays when our metadata is in a machine-actionable form, but we are beginning to explore new possibilities in the ways that we can deliver the necessary information to the user. Since driving with a map on your lap and reading it while navigating the roads is far from ideal, new map services have developed that know where you are by using global positioning. Some even speak the directions to the driver, who then can follow them without taking her eyes off the road. This is an excellent example of basing functionality

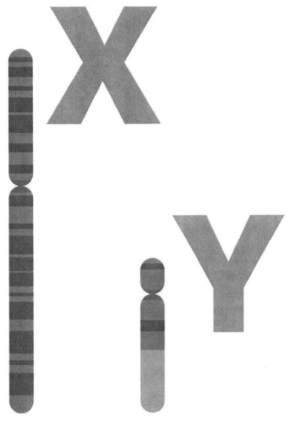

Figure 5
DNA as metadata [source: http://genomics.energy.gov].

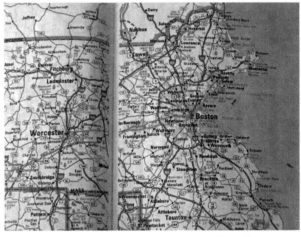

Figure 6
Printed map.

Figure 7
Online map.

Understanding the Semantic Web: Bibliographic Data and Metadata **Karen Coyle**

Library Technology Reports   www.alatechsource.org   January 2010

Figure 8
Google Map with hotels.

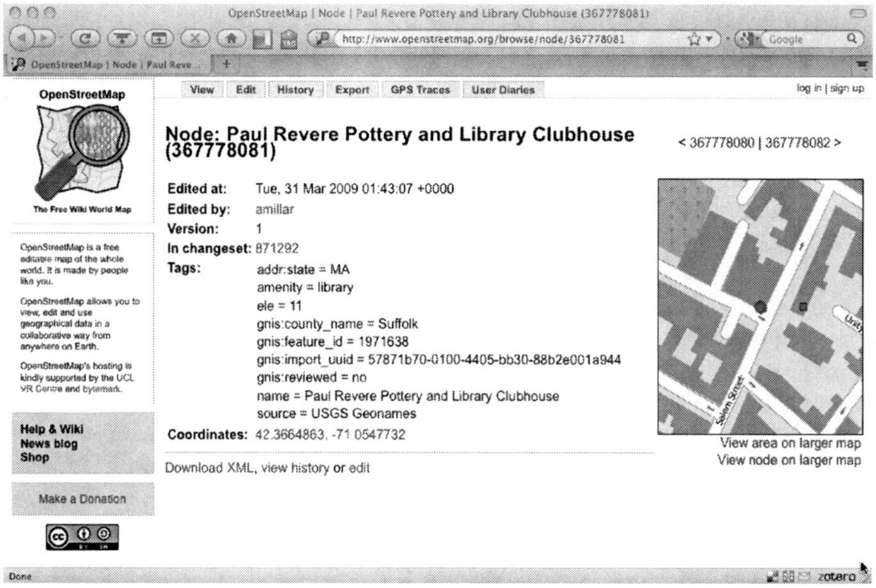

Figure 9
OpenStreetMap.org display of details.

that they can be admitted to the shelves and select their books on actual examination. As that is often not the case, a catalogue becomes necessary, and, even when it is the case, if the books are so numerous there must be some sort of guide to insure the quick finding of any particular book. The librarian can furnish some assistance, but his memory, upon which he can rely for books in general use, is of no avail for those which are sometimes wanted very much, although not wanted often.
—Charles Ammi Cutter[2]

Although the examples here are mainly about maps and navigating, the principles are the same when applied to other kinds of data, including bibliographic data. There is no question that libraries were among the earliest of social institutions to understand the function and value of metadata. There is evidence that even in the days of scroll-based libraries, some metadata was affixed to the end of each scroll on a tag that helped mark the location of the item when it was sought.[3]

Library bibliographic metadata has a number of functions: it acts as an inventory of the library's holdings; it aids in the discovery of those holdings in libraries large enough that the collection is not entirely known to the user; it acts as a surrogate for the item itself, which is often stored on a shelf with only its spine visible or in closed stacks. In addition, library cataloging practices over the years have developed methods for the identification of named persons, places, and topics.

Library metadata began as the library catalog, a finding aid for librarians and users. In the middle of the nineteenth century, the library catalog thinker like Charles Jewett had

on the needs of the user and the context in which the data will be used.

Libraries and Metadata

It is fortunate for those who have the use of a library if their number is so small and their character so high relatively limited requirements for the library catalog:

> A catalog of a library is, strictly speaking, but a list of the titles of the books, which it contains.[4]

Later in that century, Charles Ammi Cutter saw the catalog not only as a list, but as a tool for answering information questions. Cutter had a lengthy set of questions that he wished the catalog to answer:

> 1st. Has the library such a book by a certain author?
> 2nd. What books by a certain author has it?
> 3rd. Has it a book with a given title?
> 4th. Has it a certain book on a given subject?
> 5th. What books has it on a given subject?
> 6th. What books has it in a certain class of literature?
> 7th. What books have you in certain languages?

These are especially impressive because there was not a technology, beyond the book or card catalog, to help libraries provide these services. The one advantage that the developers of the library catalogs had in that day was that these were the only functions that the catalog would address, and the interface (the card) would have only human readers as its users. Our requirements became more detailed in the twentieth century, both because of the growth of libraries and the need for new technologies to serve our users and also because of the increased complexity of library management and the need to automate many library tasks.

In 1876, when Cutter wished for a catalog that would answer the question "What books have you in certain languages?" he could not have anticipated the need to filter one's retrieved set by language in order to reduce the number of items retrieved from thousands to "only" three or four hundred. It is clearly no longer sufficient to limit searches to author, title, and subject only, and successful searching is definitely not achieved solely through an alphabetical list of headings. Narrowing down a search today is as important as retrieving catalog records representing the holdings of the library.

The phenomenon of "information overload" was a fact of life before computer systems became inexpensive enough to be used in institutions like libraries. Had it not been for the computer, it is unlikely that libraries could have even begun to handle the explosion of information resources that occurred in the second half of the twentieth century. To be sure, by that time the contents of libraries had long outgrown the memory capacity of librarians.

To help users navigate this much more populous and fluid information landscape, library catalogs have been adding functionality that Cutter would not have even dreamed of. Selecting "a few good books" out of a catalog of millions of items is something no user would have the time to do. To help users get to the right resources, libraries are adding facets to narrow searches; ranking results to show users the most likely items first; adding book covers, tables of contents, and reviews that will give the user more information about the item than the facts in the catalog record; and using other techniques. Libraries have also tried to find ways to integrate their systems with the catalog information resources that have traditionally been treated as separate, such as the searching of abstracting and indexing services. All of these have put pressure on the catalog record, pushing it to perform functions it was not consciously designed to do.

Although the public catalog was designed to serve the user of the library, other information has always been used by librarians to manage the business of the library, including catalog production. Separate shelf lists and authority catalogs, rarely if ever seen by users, were an essential part of the management of libraries—especially of large libraries. Another type of catalog was used to track the receipt of serial issues, and yet another was needed for delivery and receipt of other materials. As these functions became automated, the catalog record ceased having a separate existence in the public catalog and became a part of library management systems. By the end of the twentieth century, the library record had to satisfy the needs of users, and in addition it had to provide support for a number of systems functions.

The integration of a variety of automated systems into a single library system has placed new demands on the record that represents the item held by the library, some of which are unrelated to satisfying user needs. The end result has been that the catalog record has taken on some system functions at the same time that it has had to respond to more complex user services. In addition to the purposes outlined by Cutter, library metadata has to interoperate with the library management data elements and systems functions, such as acquisitions and fund accounting, serials control and check in, and circulation systems.

Design for Sharing

The rise of a new information environment—the World Wide Web—has revealed the downside of the long history that libraries have with metadata. Library metadata methods were developed long before the advent of computer processing of metadata, and therefore library metadata, like the printed map in figure 6, was designed to be read and interpreted by human beings without any intervention by machines. It also was designed to basically stay the same throughout its existence, not to be recombined with other data.

In spite of this legacy of pre-computer practice, the question that we must face, and that we must face sooner rather than later, is how we can best transform our data so that it can become part of the dominant information environment that is the Web. This is a radical change in the context for library metadata, yet it is a logical extension of the design for sharing that has been a principle of library cataloging.

An important function of modern cataloging has been the sharing of catalogs and cataloging between libraries. The cataloging rules of the nineteenth and twentieth centuries evolved from institutional-specific rules to a modern concept of a widely used standard for sharable data that would facilitate the exchange of catalog information between libraries. In the nineteenth century, libraries printed book catalogs that could be given or sold to other libraries. Users could consult these catalogs to discover works held by other libraries. This was perhaps the first phase of remote access to library catalogs. The book catalog was portable and could be issued in multiple copies. Unfortunately, it was expensive to produce, since printing in those times meant setting type, and it quickly fell out of date. Adding new entries meant either issuing supplements outside of the order of the main catalog or reprinting the entire catalog with the new content inserted in its proper order.

The card catalog solved the update problem that the book catalog had suffered: new entries could be added anywhere in the catalog in their correct place by interfiling cards. However, the card catalog was not reproducible, so it was no longer possible to distribute copies of catalogs to other libraries.

This isolation of the library card catalog remained a problem for about one hundred years. It was only when the physical cards became electronic records in a database, and that database was connected to a global network, that libraries were able to achieve both goals: flexibility of update and remote access. Groups of libraries using the same data standards and cataloging rules were able to create union catalogs representing the holdings of multiple libraries. One such union catalog, WorldCat, has achieved the distinction as the world's largest database of library bibliographic data and holdings information.

Sharing of data among libraries has created great efficiencies in catalog production, and it has also expanded the available universe of resources for library users. Libraries remain, however, as an information environment separate from the Web. This makes a difference because the Web is where the majority of information seekers live, work, and play. It is also increasingly the environment where new information is created. Many information resources developed today will never be published in the traditional print-on-paper sense of that term. Users have less and less incentive to leave the Web and enter the library, either physically or by visiting a library catalog online.

The important question now is: how can the library catalog move from being "on the Web" to being "of the Web"? The linked data technology that has developed out of the semantic Web provides an interesting path to follow. It is specifically designed to facilitate the sharing of information on the Web, much in the way that the Web itself was developed to allow the sharing of documents. The library must become intertwined with that rich, shared, linked information space that is the Web. Rather than creating data that can be entered only into the library catalog, we need to develop a way to create data that can also be shared on the Web. This requires that we expand the context for the metadata that we create.

We are fortunate in the sense that we are in a position of having a large body of data that has been developed with sharing in mind, and also that the early developers of library cataloging codes, such as Anthony Panizzi, understood the value of consistency and the application of rules. Because of this situation, we are better positioned than some professions to redefine our data to be used in a complex and rich data environment such as the World Wide Web.

The Web as Context

The library catalog has been the sole context for library data since its inception. It is not a coincidence that we call the creation of library bibliographic data "cataloging," that is, the creation of the catalog. The result has been a uniform set of metadata designed for the catalog's purposes: identifying the library's holdings, supporting management of those holdings, and providing entry and discovery points for librarians and nonlibrarian users.

There is an unmistakable need for libraries to know what they own as well as the current whereabouts of each item in their inventory, and the catalog is the basis for these functions. The use of the library catalog by information seekers, however, is diminishing, by all accounts. When journal article information became available online as a library service, users jumped at the chance to have easy access to this data, and soon more searches were being done in these databases than in the library's traditional catalog.[6] It's not that one resource replaces the other, but that users have a finite amount of time and attention; new information sources that gain favor take up a certain quantity of the users' information-seeking energies. Regardless of the inherent value of library-owned materials, there are only twenty-four hours in a day, and the time for study, research, and recreation does not expand as more information becomes available. The famed "information overload" is a time problem.

For a variety of reasons, users favor the Web as an information platform over the library. Studies show that users like the simple search options, and in particular they are pleased by the instant gratification that moves them directly from search to resources without having to even move their fingers from the keyboard. They also find great value in the social aspects of the Web, not so much for finding dates for Friday night, but in getting an idea of which resources might be best for them. One can question the quality of the ranking that users are presented with, but rather than face many screens of undifferentiated results, users are grateful that Internet search engines give them ranked results. The ranking is based on algorithms that are trade secrets, but the user knows that the first page is what nearly "everyone" would consider to be the key resources for their keyword query. When looking for a "good read," a search on Amazon will turn up the best sellers out of the retrieved set. Services like Facebook, YouTube, and Flickr all allow users to create and view popularity ratings for resources and to write comments and reviews. All of these help users select from among a large number of retrieved items.

There are a number of social networking sites organized around books, such as LibraryThing, Goodreads, and BookMooch, each a kind of MySpace for the bookish set. In some cases the data has been derived from library bibliographic records, but it is just as likely to have come from nonlibrary sources such as Amazon.com. Amazon gets its data from publishers and booksellers, not from libraries. Some sites, such as Google Book Search, combine data from a variety of different sources, merging some descriptive data from libraries with the marketing data received from publishers (blurbs, author biographies).

Across these sites and many others, the Web is virtually awash in bibliographic data, and users who frequent certain Web sites are accustomed to seeing bibliographic data in contexts far from the library catalog. The *New York Times* bestseller list is online, as are the Web sites of publishers and authors. Libraries may have the greatest number of titles and the rare materials, but there is plenty of overlap in content between the library and Web, and between the library catalog and information on the Web. In addition, there is nonbibliographic data that could be related to bibliographic data. For example, the name "Herman Melville" and the fact that he wrote *Moby Dick* are facts that are not limited to the data in library catalogs; it is also found in encyclopedias, online discussions of American literature, and the course reading lists of classes of colleges and universities that can be found online.

Although there is an overlap of data, there is very little direct connection between the library catalog and the Web. Bibliographic citations online, such as those in the reference sections of Wikipedia entries, may link to a library's holdings. For example, if you retrieve bibliographic data, perhaps on Google, Open Library, or Goodreads, that represents a book, you can use that as a launch point to find the book in a library by using WorldCat. You can't, however, move easily from a statement in an essay about Abraham Lincoln to a list of books about Lincoln, much less a list of relevant books in your local library (let alone a list of resources that are on the shelf and currently available). Imagine if an online search on J. K. Rowling or Harry Potter could become an entry point into the library, and the visibility that could provide for libraries.

In return, library data could enrich bibliographic entries on the Web. Libraries are the only community with control over names, distinguishing between authors with the same or similar names and bringing together variant name forms. The addition of birth and death dates, once needed only to disambiguate similar names, is now essential information for an analysis of copyright status. Library data also facilitates the gathering of different editions around the concept of a work through the use of uniform titles. All told, the data that exists today in library catalogs could enhance the Web.

Change Happens

The need to change does not mean that what you are doing is wrong. Instead, it often means that something in your environment has changed, something that you cannot control. The change addressed by library cataloging pioneers like Panizzi and Cutter was that as the rate of publishing was greatly increasing, scholars and readers could no longer know everything that was available. The catalog was needed to help these users. At one time, the idea of a search by topic was unheard of, but it became necessary for catalogs to address so that users could find unknown items without help of librarian ("Give me a good book on . . ."). The change that we must address is that the Web is increasingly the source of information for searchers and researchers, and that the library needs to be interconnected with that web of data.

Library Technology Reports   www.alatechsource.org   January 2010

Notes

1. Great Britain, Parliament, *Parliamentary Papers (Commons), 31 January–15 August 1850*, vol. 33 (*Accounts and Papers*, vol. 1), No. 425, 1850, "Communications Addressed to the Treasury by the Trustees of the British Museum, With Reference to the Report of the Commissioners Appointed to Inquire Into the Constitution and Management of the British Museum," 247, quoted in Jon R. Hufford, "The Pragmatic Basis of Catalog Codes: Has the User Been Ignored?" Texas Tech University, Libraries Faculty Research, 2007, http://dspace.lib.ttu.edu/bitstream/handle/2346/510/fulltext.pdf?sequence=1 (accessed Nov. 28, 2009).

2. Charles Ammi Cutter, "Library Catalogues," in *Public Libraries in the United States of America. Their History, Condition, and Management: Special Report, Department of the Interior, Bureau of Education, Part I*, 526–622 (Washington, DC: Government Printing Office, 1876), 526.

3. Charles Jewett, quoted in Henry Petroski: Henry Petroski, *The Book on the Bookshelf*, 1st ed. (New York: Alfred A. Knopf, 1999), 28.

4. Charles Coffin Jewett, *On the Construction of Catalogues of Libraries*, 2nd ed. (Washington, DC: Smithsonian Institution, 1853), 10.

5. Cutter, "Library Catalogues," 527.

6. Rosalie Lack and John Ober, *California Digital Library: Key Indicators of Collections and Use, July 1, 2001–June 30, 2002.* (Oakland, CA: California Digital Library, 2002). Available at www.cdlib.org/about/publications/fy01-02cdl_statsprofile.pdf (accessed Nov. 28, 2009).

Chapter 2

Changing the Nature of Library Data

Chapter Abstract

In our current technology environment, all information goes through computers before reaching a human being, so it is necessary to design our metadata to be data—that is, to give it the ability to be manipulated by computer programs. To keep pace with modern advances in technology, the library catalog data must be transformed from being primarily a textual description to a set of data elements to which machine processes can be applied; and these data elements must be compatible with the current mainstream technology that is the World Wide Web. This chapter of "Understanding the Semantic Web: Bibliographic Data and Metadata" examines what steps the library community will need to take to facilitate this transformation.

Change can be difficult, and change within long-standing communities of practice can be particularly difficult. The first hurdle is recognizing that change is necessary. The next is to understand the nature of the change: its goals, its possibilities, and the natural limitations that will inevitably move the effort from an ideal solution to a more realistic one. The last challenge is to arrive at an agreement within the community on a change that will return a good value for the effort it requires.

Among librarians, there has already been a realization that a change is needed when it comes to how libraries present their catalog data. This has been a topic of study and action for well over a decade. Such thinking produced a new model for bibliographic data, the Functional Requirements for Bibliographic Data (FRBR), and a proposed new rule set for cataloging practice, Resource Description and Access (RDA).

Together these provide a new conceptual foundation but leave us with a key piece missing: how to express our data in a twenty-first-century data format. For this we are given some direction in the report of the Working Group on the Future of Bibliographic Control:

> **Desired Outcomes:** Library bibliographic data will move from the closed database model to the open Web-based model wherein records are addressable by programs and are in formats that can be easily integrated into Web services and computer applications. This will enable libraries to make better use of networked data resources and to take advantage of the relationships that exist (or could be made to exist) among various data sources on the Web.[1]

The report does not say how library data must change to make this mandate a reality. There will surely be more than one way to accomplish this goal, but a few things are certain: the library catalog data must be transformed from being primarily a textual description to a set of data elements to which machine processes can be applied; and these data elements must be compatible with the current mainstream technology that is the World Wide Web. One possible direction for library data is to join the linked data "cloud," a growing set of data on the World Wide Web that many see as having great promise for a richer information future.

From Metadata to MetaDATA

In our current technology environment, all information goes through computers before reaching a human being, so it is necessary to design our metadata to be data—that is, to give it the ability to be manipulated by computer

Library Technology Reports   www.alatechsource.org   January 2010

programs. In a sense, we did this with the MARC record in the 1960s, but at that time the capabilities for processing data were much, much less advanced than they are today. It was a time before keyword searching, before data mining, and before the concept that information from a wide variety of heterogeneous sources would all intermingle over a single, large network, the Internet.

Libraries were among the first institutions to use computers to process text. In the 1960s, when the MARC format was introduced, it was extremely unusual to process fields of variable length and to process text as it is normally written, using both upper- and lowercase, punctuation, and even accented characters. Libraries developed ways to create mixed character sets with both Latin and non-Latin characters years before other communities found the need to do so. We are no longer alone, however, in our need to process and manipulate text. The development of Unicode, a single character set for all known languages and scripts, and XML, a data format that is flexible enough to describe very complex texts, have brought us into a world where text processing is no longer the exception in the computing world.

Today's data design has to balance the functionality needed for machine processing with the understandable information format needs of the human end user. It is definitely not a matter of serving only the machine or only the human reader, but of creating data that can serve both. Compromises will often have to be made. The current version of library data, however, is not serving the machine functionality well, so our challenge is to bring our data into the twenty-first century for machine processing and to improve service to our human end users by being able to offer more functionality in our systems. This report presents a sample of some steps that can be taken to accomplish this goal, but please keep in mind that this is not a complete recipe for the future of library data, just some of the ingredients.

Data-fy the Data

The library catalog record is mainly a textual document. It is true that this text is coded in fields and subfields in the machine-readable record, but the physical basis of the record is still primarily text. In essence, the MARC record can be considered one of the first text markup languages, if not *the* first. The record has some fields with coded data that were designed for the machine processing of that era, which needed data to be stored at a fixed length and with its contents as compact as possible. When the MARC format was developed in the 1960s, the difference between the storage of "eng" versus "English" to describe the language of a work was significant in terms of system capabilities. The fixed-field data overcomes some of the "text-ness" of the primary bibliographic data. For example, the date of publication in the publication statement can take different forms, such as:

1966 (a simple date)

c1966 (a copyright date)

[1966] (a date supplied by cataloger)

[1966?] (a date supplied by cataloger and uncertain)

In the fixed-field area, the format of the data is strictly controlled as four characters, generally numeric. Each of these would be coded there as "1966":

740813s1966 enkcf b 000 0aeng

The punctuation and other information in the date field, while perhaps useful to human readers (at least to those who know what they mean), are an impediment to machine processing.

Many of the key fields of the bibliographic record, however, are not available in a data format. One example is the ISBN, a very important element in a number of library operations, from acquisitions to linking cover images with the user interface. The ISBN is stored in a subfield in the MARC record, but that subfield can contain other information in textual form:

9781416554950 (trade pbk.)

0817315497 (cloth : alk. Paper)

0415981484 (Hardcover : alk. Paper)

0847829413 (hbk.)

080327946X :

Although it is possible to select the ISBN itself from this string using programming algorithms,* and all systems that use the ISBN in processing must do so, there seems to be little reason not to provide the ISBN in a form that can readily be manipulated by machines, since that is how it will be used. What causes libraries to continue with practices that aren't appropriate to this day and age? Habit, and the very important fact that a large body of legacy data is a reflection of those practices.

While the use of a data field for a particular data element may be a solution to the problem of text versus data, one of the results is that many data elements in library records are entered more than once in the same record, in slightly different formats. It is well known in the world of information technology that any time you store the same information in more than one place, you risk those sepa-

---

As an example, this is a line of code from the Open Library project (http://openlibrary.org) that extracts the ISBN from the MARC subfield using a regular expression: re_isbn = re.compile('([^ ()]+[\dX])(?: \((?:v\. \(\d+)(?: :)?)?(.)\))?')

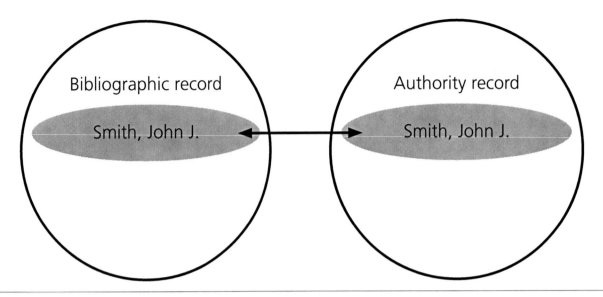

Figure 10
Sample bibliographic and name records, linked.

rate versions of the data falling out of sync. For example, someone may discover that the date has been entered incorrectly in a record, as "c1964" instead of "c1965." That person may correct the display form of the data in the publication statement, but could easily forget that there is also a coded form in the fixed-field area. Adding to this possibility is the fact that in all systems that I have seen, these two data elements are not near each other in the user interface used by the cataloger.

The method of adding some data fields to what is essentially a textual document (the catalog entry) may have been appropriate in the middle of the twentieth century, but twenty-first-century computing provides us with better solutions. Those solutions allow for the coding of data for machine use without sacrificing service to the human user. The use of authority-controlled headings in library data is a good example of where a small change in how we store our data could greatly increase the machine capabilities in relation to library records.

Identify the Data

Some of the information in the library record will, of necessity, be text. The concept of authority and control and headings in library data, however, means that even many of the text fields are not simply free text but have structure and are controlled as to their content. These headings are often the primary access points that correspond to the information that users have when they approach the library: authors, titles, and subjects. There are separate records in our systems for some of these elements, records that contain additional information needed to provide entry vocabulary for the user and to

help catalogers create library data with a certain level of consistency. This isn't as useful as it could be in automated systems because the connection between the heading in the bibliographic record and that in the authority record are made on the basis of the display text in the fields. Should the display text change, the link between these two elements is broken, and systems cannot bring them together. This loss of connection between the bibliographic and the name authority data can be remedied by making use of identifiers that can be read by machines. Both bibliographic and authority records can contain this identifier, and the display text can be changed as needed without breaking the link. In other words, one links through identifiers, not through display text. Say that you have bibliographic and name records that need to link, and what they have in terms of data is shown in figure 10.

If the name record changes, nothing links the two any more, as shown in figure 11, because the display form has changed, and the display form was also the linking string.

If one uses identifiers for names, in addition to the display forms and other common references in a name authority record, as shown in figure 12, display forms can change without breaking the link between the records. The bibliographic record now needs to update its display form, but it can do so using the shared identifier. Although the two records are showing different display forms, the link between them is not broken.

In addition, some areas of our data may appear the same in display, but have different coding in the underlying data record. Because of this difference in coding, they will be considered different by machines. For example, the data elements of what libraries call a "main entry" (usually a person or corporate body that creates a resource)

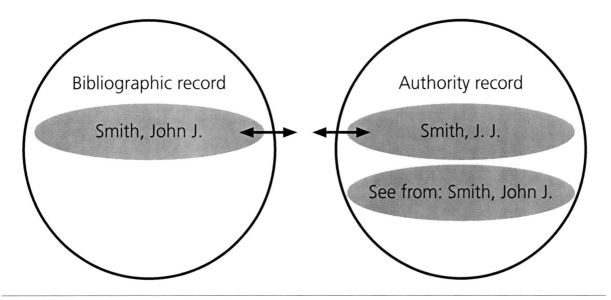

Figure 11
Sample bibliographic and name records; link broken due to name change.

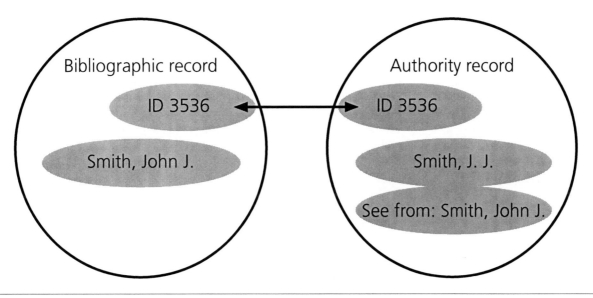

Figure 12
Sample bibliographic and name records with identifiers; links remain.

are subdivided into numerous subfields in one part of the library record, but given as a single string in other areas of the record. Sometimes the type of entity is specified (person, corporate body), other times it is not. These inconsistencies are not visible in the user display of the bibliographic data, but if the data is to be used consistently in automated functions, these differences need to be overcome. Some of them can be overcome with programming, and some, unfortunately, cannot. The use of identifiers for the intended text forms removes the ambiguity for machine processing and allows algorithms to

know immediately when the bibliographic data is referring to a particular name entry.

Exit the Database

In the latter half of the twentieth century, the primary data model was that of the database, and in particular the relational database. Nearly all systems that made use of the data in libraries used database management systems. The primarily textual nature of the library bibliographic record made it less suitable for the kind of organization that database management systems do best. Database technology was designed for a different kind of data, less textual and more compact, with fewer data elements and less of a range of content in those elements. Database technology is designed to retrieve. For example, it can retrieve all of the invoices that contain a particular product code. Database management systems work best in environments with a lot of repetition of data values.

Library data is less data-like than the business data for which database management systems were designed. For example, most titles of works are unique, and most authors appear only once in any given database. Much of the efficiency of database management is lost when working with data of this type. It is also difficult to make use of some of the features of database management systems, at least in a way that would be efficient. Library data was designed to be ordered alphabetically by very long text strings, something that database management systems do fairly poorly. Similarly, the systems often have limits in terms of the length of a string that they can index. Keyword indexing opened up a whole new way to access bibliographic data, but the vast number of individual keywords that the catalog of a large, multilingual library collection will produce can easily overwhelm a traditional business database product.

In addition, the record format that we are using, MARC, is unlike the format of any other community, and that means that those creating library systems have to write specific programs to make the data fit in the standard business database world. It is rather ironic, but our data is so much more textually sophisticated than most business data that we simply cannot use standard business software in our systems. Library systems have to be built from the ground up, taking a great deal of system developer resources and adding to the cost of the systems.

Today, many more communities produce and manipulate sophisticated textual data in a machine-readable form, and the technology has been developed to make working with that data easier. We now have the means to design and store our data that are not limited to libraries, but are part of the mainstream of computing. The creation of an XML format for MARC, using Unicode, is a step toward the transformation of library-specific data into something that could be used by anyone, anywhere in an information system. The problem, as has been noted by many, is that MARC is still primarily a textual document,[2] and MARCXML provides the kind of markup of that text that would guide displays. A more radical transformation of library data is necessary if we are to move from database-managed search and display into an interactive use of library data on the Web. Why on the Web? The answer is rather simple: because that's where our users are. In addition, that is also where many people are creating and working with bibliographic data, and they are doing so without the benefit of the great wealth of bibliographic knowledge that has already been by created in libraries.

Semantic Web, Linked Data, and Other New Technologies

As is often the case, each era has a technology trend that is put forward as the solution to every problem. In fact, these technology trends usually have merit in spite of the surplus of hype that surrounds them. In addition, the hype almost never mentions any defects or downsides of the currently hyped concept. The important thing is to look beyond the hype to the actual value that the technology provides, and to what the technology can be *in practice*. Every new technology solves some problems, but not all of them, and there is always some room for improvement. This is certainly the case in this moment in time. The Semantic Web is currently the "flavor of the month" as far as technology goes.

The basic concept behind the Semantic Web is not as mysterious as it sounds. Today's Web is a web of documents that link to each other. This was the idea that led Tim Berners-Lee to create the World Wide Web: the need for scientists to put their documents on the Internet and to create links so that the documents could link to one another, thus creating a web of documentation, not unlike the famed memex of Vannevar Bush.[3] The links generally go from a point in one document to another document, with some pages consisting almost entirely of links that serve as entry points to collections. The links themselves, however, are not very informative: they have no meaning beyond *link*. They do not explain why you have linked, nor what the link itself could mean. A link could be a citation that supports a quote, it could be document that gives further information, or it could be critical ("Whatever you do, don't believe what this person says here!"). Note also that links go in only one direction, so a document that has links to it is not aware of those links. Such links can sometimes be discovered through search engines, but the Web itself does not provide for their easy discovery or use.

At the time that he "invented" the Web, Tim Berners-Lee's online world was a very narrow one of researchers at the European Organization for Nuclear Research (CERN) in Geneva. It is probable that at that time he had no idea of the types of information resources that might eventually be found on the Web, resources that have nothing to do with scientific papers. There is almost no type of human endeavor that you can't find today on the Web, and it has evolved into a somewhat messy, heterogeneous source of information of all kinds.

Web pages take forms that have little if anything to do with the format and content of a scientific article. What is clear, though, is that there is a lot of information on the Web that is embedded in text. This text is the object of search engines, which extract words so that Internet users can find the pages or texts based on the words within them. This is very different from the library catalog, which creates an entirely new text—a catalog record—to represent the actual content of the document. Web searching operates directly on the text of the document itself. But in many ways, words are problematic as information resources. They can be ambiguous (e.g., Pluto the Disney character versus Pluto the orbiting body). They can be incomplete informationally, since many concepts require more than one word (e.g., solar energy, ancient Rome). They are language-based, so a search on *computer* does not bring up documents with the term *ordinateur*. And of course keyword searching falls prey to differences in spelling (fiber versus fibre) and errors in spelling or typography (history versus histroy).

All of this could lead one to conclude that something else is needed, something that helps us find information in the great wealth of expression that is the World Wide Web. For this, Tim Berners-Lee and colleagues at the World Wide Web Consortium have proposed the Semantic Web as one solution.[4] The Semantic Web would, in essence, make it possible to mine the World Wide Web for information that can be found within the many pages of the Web. It creates a new layer on the World Wide Web, a web of information found in the web of documents. Essentially, the idea is to evolve from a web of documents that link to each other to a way to connect, search, and make use of data in those documents.

To do this, it is necessary to be more precise in how we code certain parts of our texts. In particular, we need ways to make our texts more usable by machines. It may seem obvious to a person reading a text that a statement like this one:

> Herman Melville was an American author in the mid-1800s and wrote numerous literary works, among which the most famous is *Moby Dick*, a book based in the whaling culture of New England.

that the facts contained in here are

- Herman Melville was an American.
- Herman Melville was an author.
- Herman Melville is no longer alive.
- Herman Melville wrote *Moby Dick*.
- *Moby Dick* is a book.
- Herman Melville wrote other things as well.
- *Moby Dick*, the book, has something to do with whaling and New England.
- *Moby Dick*, the book, is famous.

Unfortunately, none of this is understood by a computer, nor can one easily program a computer to retrieve these facts from the text as understood by a person. Teaching computers to understand simple utterances has been the goal of the discipline of artificial intelligence for over half a century, with disappointing results. The idea of the Semantic Web is to make it possible to identify the data in Web documents and make that data usable as a web of information.

It might occur to the reader at this point that library catalog records do contain some of the inferences listed above in a coded form. In fact, library data could help the Web understand its own hidden data. To do so, however, it will be necessary to follow Semantic Web standards for data formats. First, we need to understand what the underlying structures of the Semantic Web are.

Semantic Web

The Semantic Web is about metadata designed to be used by computers. The fact that this is called "semantic" is more than a little confusing since we know that computers are totally a-semantic—that is, that they can calculate, move, rearrange, and sort, but totally lack understanding. They have what Bruce Sterling has termed "the truly profound stupidity of the inanimate."[5] The commonly understood definition of *semantics* is "meaning of words." That is not the case with the Semantic Web. The Semantic Web uses the term as it is defined in an area of mathematics known as formal languages. For example, computer programming languages use formal semantics that define the set of possible computations that the language can perform, like addition, subtraction, and division. In this sense of the term, *semantics* means a calculatable syntax, such as:

> if A = B, and A = C, then B = C

In formal languages, you model rules that allow you to determine if something is or is not true within the definitions of the model. The result is a mathematical truth, not a human semantic truth, and what the computer does has nothing at all to do with any meaning that humans may impart to A, B, or C. If the data read

> ANIMAL = DOG and ANIMAL = CAT

the formal language would conclude

> Therefore DOG = CAT

This is obviously a false statement to a human reader (and one that both cats and dogs would find insulting), but it would be true to the computer under the rules of its language. This serves, therefore, as an illustration of another well-known computing concept: GIGO, or "garbage in, garbage out." The computer will perform its operations even when the data itself is absurd, and it will be unaware of the absurdity. Quality results come only from

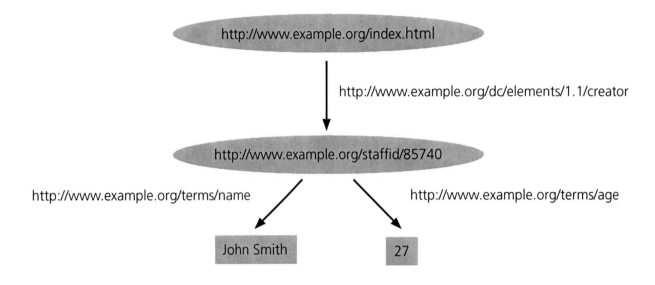

Figure 13
From Frank Manola and Eric Miller, eds., "RDF Primer," World Wide Web Consortium website, Feb. 10, 2004, fig. 4, www. w3.org/TR/2004/REC-rdf-primer-20040210/#figure4 (accessed Nov. 17, 2009). Copyright © 2004 World Wide Web Consortium (Massachusetts Institute of Technology, European Research Consortium for Informatics and Mathematics, Keio University). All Rights Reserved. http://www.w3.org/Consortium/Legal/2002/copyright-documents-20021231.

quality data, and quality data has meaning in the human sense. Computers perform operations based on rules, not on meaning in the human sense of that term.

The data model for the Semantic Web is defined in the documentation for the Resource Description Framework (RDF). RDF is devilishly difficult to understand in its formal, mathematical definition, but is actually quite simple at a conceptual level. It defines a set of rules for the formal semantics of metadata that is meant for the elements and structure of metadata that will be able to operate on the Semantic Web. Very simply put, in the Semantic Web all data consists of things and relationships between them, with the smallest unit being a statement of the form:

a thing → with relationship to → another thing

This is of course an oversimplification, but it is the basic concept to keep in mind when working with data in this new environment. You may see this concept expressed using diagrams, such as the one shown in figure 13, from the RDF Primer document:

The Semantic Web elements and rules are simple, yet, like atoms, they can be combined into very complex working units. Some of the basic components are resources and classes, properties, and values.

Resources

The Semantic Web does not limit what it can describe. Essentially any thing or concept can be part of a Semantic Web statement. Even relationships can be considered *things*. To talk about the Semantic Web in a general way,

documents (and users) tend to use the term *resource* as a neutral way of referring to what Semantic Web statements can be about.

Classes, Properties, and Values

It is easy to define the three Semantic Web terms *classes*, *properties*, and *values* by using analogous terms from information technology, but be aware that the Semantic Web has very specific definitions that go beyond the common understanding of these terms.

Classes

A *class* is much like a class in a scientific taxonomic sense: it is a grouping of like resources that all belong together based on some common characteristics that make them members of the same set. An example of a class is "vehicles," where members of the class are "cars," "trains," and "planes." But you could also define a class called "things I own," and this class can include "car," "computer," and "dog." In other words, there isn't a universal class, just the classes that are useful for your metadata.

Properties

A *property* is what we often think of as a data element in metadata. It's an element of description for the resources

Links to W3C's documents on RDF
www.w3.org/RDF

Understanding the Semantic Web: Bibliographic Data and Metadata   **Karen Coyle**

your metadata addresses. If your metadata describes cars on a car lot, then properties can be "model," "color," and "price." If our class is "books in a library," then we will have properties like "title," "subject," "location," and "accession number."

Values

Value as defined in RDF is the actual content of the data element. So if "color" is a property, then "Dyno blue pearl" is a value—at least it is when you are creating metadata for a Honda Civic. When it comes to library materials, where "title" is a property, values will be things like "Harry Potter and the Chamber of Secrets," "Brave new world," and "5 piano concertos."

An important concept in the area of values is that of uncontrolled and controlled values. The Semantic Web uses the terms "literal" and "non-literal" for these, but I will use the more common library terminology here for the sake of communication. These concepts are ones that the library world has embraced since the beginning of modern cataloging practice, but are newly discovered for some nonlibrary communities that are creating metadata for the first time.

In library metadata we have some fields that can take any string of characters. Among these are the title, various notes, and other fields whose content is mainly textual and unpredictable. These fields therefore have uncontrolled values in them. Many fields, however, including some fields that are textual in nature, have controlled values. All of the fields that comprise the catalog record's headings are in some way or another under control. They are often taken from authority records, where a decision has been made as to the preferred display and its format. Other fields, primarily the coded fields in the MARC record, select from a list of possible values, such as the codes for "music form of composition" or "target audience." These elements have a finite list that catalogers must choose from.

Values may also be controlled as to form as well as to content. Library data has few of these, but may embrace more as catalog metadata becomes more data-like. For example, metadata often restricts the format of date and time so that it can be processed by a machine. The MARC21 record does this in the 005 field, where the date and time are recorded according to "Numeric Representation of Dates and Times" as defined by the standard ISO 8601, the international standard covering the exchange of date- and time-related data.[6] The standard defines the structure of the data element (YYYY-MM-DD, where Y is a year digit, M is a month digit, and D is a day digit) and exactly which characters are valid for each portion of the date. Other structured elements, although less obviously so, are the ISBN, which has a language group segment, publisher segment, and a book segment; and the LCCN, formatted as the year followed by an accession number.

Identification and URIs

A key element of the Semantic Web is to identify our things and relationships in a way that can be understood by machines. This means that every thing that we wish to work with has to have an identifier that distinguishes it from any other thing. There are many kinds of identifiers, from plain numbers to complex alphanumeric strings. The primary rule for the Semantic Web is that identifiers need to be in the form of a Uniform Resource Identifier, which is a particular form of identifier. We don't need to go into the structure of URIs because it turns out that the common Uniform Resource Locator, URL, is in URI format and is the preferred identifier to use on the Semantic Web. This means that URLs can be used as identifiers as well as locations, which can sometimes be confusing. Among the advantages of using URLs, however, is that they can easily be used to return information about the thing being identified using HTTP (Hypertext Transfer Protocol). HTTP is used by browsers and other programs to retrieve documents on the Web and therefore needs no additional programming for this approach to work. In the case of an identifier, what you might retrieve is a description of what is being identified, whereas when the URL is a location, you are directed to the document or to a site that is at that location.

Tim Berners-Lee, the "father of the World Wide Web" and one of the primary originators of the concepts of the Semantic Web, says this about the use of URIs:

> An information object is "on the Web" if it has a URI. Objects which have URIs are sometimes known as "First Class Objects" (FCOs). The Web works best when any information object of value and identity is a first class object. If something does not have a URI, you can't refer to it, and the power of the Web is the less for that.[7]

The URI is what allows a resource to be a thing on the Web and to be actionable on the Web. If you want to link to something, it has to have a URI. If you want to locate it, it has to have a URL (which is also a URI). To give library metadata a presence on the Web, we will have to first give it an identity, in the form of a URI.

Identification actually takes place on two levels, that of the property (i.e., data element) and where possible, the values.

Properties are identified along with a definition of their meaning (in human terms) and any rules that are applied to the use of the property. For example, the Dublin Core (DC) community has created identifiers that begin with http://purl.org/dc/terms/ for each of the DC terms, and includes definitions for each of the terms at that site. Some terms, such as http://purl.org/dc/terms/date, specify the type of value that can be used with the term, in this case, values in the form of ISO 8601.

There is not currently a standard for the definition of properties. The requirement that they be RDF-compliant imposes some constraints, but displays of property definitions on the Web can vary. Here is one example of such a display for the term "title" from the Dublin Core Metadata Terms:[8]

Term Name: title

URI: http://purl.org/dc/terms/title

Label: Title

Definition: A name given to the resource.

Type of Term: Property

Refines: http://purl.org/dc/elements/1.1/title

Version: http://dublincore.org/usage/terms/history/#titleT-001

As of December 2007, the DCMI Usage Board is leaving this range unspecified pending an investigation of options.

While not exactly a thrilling read, the basic information is in understandable text. In contrast, the machine-actionable form of the term named title looks like this:

```
<rdf:Description rdf:about="http://purl.org/dc/terms/title">

    <rdfs:label xml:lang="en-US">Title</rdfs:label>

    <dcterms:description xml:lang="en-US">A name given to the resource.</dcterms:description>

    <rdfs:isDefinedBy rdf:resource="http://purl.org/dc/terms/"/><dcterms:issued>2008-01-14</dcterms:issued><dcterms:modified>2008-01-14</dcterms:modified>

    <rdf:type rdf:resource="http://www.w3.org/1999/02/22-rdf-syntax-ns#Property"/>

    <dcterms:hasVersion rdf:resource="http://dublincore.org/usage/terms/history/#titleT-001"/>

    <skos:note xml:lang="en-US">
```

In current practice, this term is used primarily with

literal values; however, there are important uses with non-literal values as well.* As of December 2007, the DCMI Usage Board is leaving this range unspecified pending an investigation of options.

```
    </skos:note>

    <rdfs:subPropertyOf rdf:resource="http://purl.org/dc/elements/1.1/title"/>

</rdf:Description>
```

In some cases, what data will populate a field is unpredictable, such as with titles, tables of contents, or free-form notes. In other cases, when the values for a property come from a controlled list, such as a list of language codes, each value can be represented by either a string of text or a URI. For example, a list of colors could be defined this way:

red

yellow

blue

The list would be identified with a URI, such as http://example.com/colorList, and anyone using that list would identify the list using the URI. For greater precision, each color could have its own URI:

http://example.com/colorList/1

http://example.com/colorList/2

http://example.com/colorList/3

For these identifiers to be useful, they need to be documented, preferably in both a machine-actionable and a human-readable form, as we saw above with the Dublin Core definition of "title." Documentation can include definitions and display forms, and both preferred and alternate displays. One important advantage of the use of identifiers, rather than natural language, is that the documentation can include display forms and other information in any number of languages.

```
http://example.com/colorList/1
<label lang=en> red
<label lang=fr> rouge
<label lang=jp> 赤
<label lang=de> Röte
```

Applications can then use the language appropriate to their audience.

---

*Note that the Dublin Core community uses the RDF terminology of "literal" and "non-literal" in its documentation.

Creation of URIs for some of the many controlled lists used in library catalog data has begun. The Library of Congress has created a site for the identification of the value lists under its control at http://id.loc.gov and has defined over three hundred thousand entries from the Library of Congress Subject Heading list. In anticipation of future Semantic Web usage, all properties, relationships and value lists related to the Resource Description and Access (RDA) rules have been registered in an RDF-compatible format and given unique identifiers under the domain http://RDVocab.org. These are therefore now available to be used in Web applications that conform to the Semantic Web data format.

Creating and Using Identifiers

The fact that some string of characters identifies some thing does not necessarily make it a good identifier. There are many poor identifiers in use—identifiers that will not last as long as the thing they identify, that are not unique in the environment in which they are being used, or that have been misapplied in practice. When working with identifiers, one must answer some basic questions in order to find the appropriate identifier and use it wisely. Among these questions are

- What does the identifier actually identify?
- Who created the identifier, and is that creator the appropriate authority for my purpose?
- What is the maintenance commitment for the identifier?
- What is the context within which this identifier is unique?
- How trustworthy is the identifier?

I'll use a very common identifier, the ISBN, to illustrate the issues these questions bring up.

- **What does the ISBN identify?** It identifies a particular product from a particular publisher. When the product changes significantly (and especially if that changes what physical object the publisher will actually move around the planet or its price), the publisher creates a different ISBN for that new product. The ISBN has some standards that address how one defines "new product" so there is some consistency across publishers, but obviously also some variance. For digital books, there is disagreement among publishers on how to use the ISBN properly and whether book publishers must assign separate ISBNs for each e-book format.
- **Who created the identifier?** The ISBN is assigned to the product by the publisher that is producing and distributing the product. The publisher is the correct one to make this decision. In addition, the ISBN is

an industry standard and is managed by a series of agencies around the world. It has standards for application.

- **What is the maintenance commitment?** This is not made explicit. Since the ISBN is printed on book covers and often also on the verso of the title page, the identifier will endure as long as there is a copy of the book in existence. For e-books, it isn't clear if or how the ISBN will be associated with the book product over time.
- **In what context is the ISBN a unique identifier?** The ISBN is unique within the work flow of the book trade. However, because the ISBN is merely a set of digits (with the occasional X in the check digit place) it must always be clearly identified as an ISBN to be considered unique. In a larger context, such as a warehouse database with many product numbers, the ISBN could easily be confused with another identifier. In a library database, an ISBN could overlap with another identifier, like the OCLC number. On the open Web, the ISBN definitely would have little use if not coded as an ISBN.

The Internet Engineering Task Force (IETF) has designated a "name space" for the ISBN that takes the URN format: urn:isbn:<isbn string>.[9] A name space is a unique naming area that can be used only for that entity. In this way, the ISBN can be moved freely around the Internet without losing its identity. That's the good news. The bad news is that URNs are not commonly used in the real Web, so most applications have their own designator for the ISBN, and there are different forms in use. In other words, we do not have a consistent way to treat ISBNs as identifiers on the Web.

- **How trustworthy is the ISBN?** Anyone who has worked with large bodies of bibliographic data has seen some of the problems of misapplied ISBNs. The vast majority of ISBNs work as designed: they identify a particular publisher product. There are cases where the wrong ISBN is assigned to a book or the wrong ISBN is entered into the metadata for a book. I have personally seen cases where a publisher, generally a very small publisher, reuses ISBNs. What this means is that for some functions, it may be necessary to use another data element, such as the title of the book, in addition to the ISBN as a way to catch these erroneous identifiers.

In all systems, there will be internal identifiers—which are often never seen by users of the system—that have meaning only within that system. As part of its functioning, a database management system assigns internal identifiers to every table and every field. These are rarely useful for anything other than the internal workings of that system. The identifiers that interest us for metadata are those that will have use in a larger context. Returning to our ISBN example, the ISBN is used throughout the book publishing supply chain, from the publisher to the individual bookstore. It has the advantage of being well known and available through a number of sources.

Links to registered RDA element sets and value vocabularies
http://metadataregistry.org/rdabrowse.htm

As we move into a more data-focused Web, agencies that maintain data are being encouraged to create identifiers for their data and controlled vocabularies. It should be the maintenance agency that provides the identifier, and the identifier should be given a name that only that agency can provide. This is why this practice is advisable for agencies that use their registered domain name as the first part of the identifier. Because no two agencies can own the same domain name on the Web, the identifier is guaranteed to be unique in that context. Two agencies that have identifiers that are six-digit numbers would create identifiers that look like this:

http://agency1.com/123456

http://agency2.com/123456

Without the domain names, the numeric identifiers would be the same, even though they point to entirely different things within the agencies' schemes. With the domain names, each one is unique.

A controversial area of identifiers is whether it is best for them to be semantically meaningful to humans or not. An example of a meaningful identifier is the one used by Wikipedia for its articles. The URL that identifies the article includes the words used in the title of the article, and therefore is somewhat understandable to a person:

http://en.wikipedia.org/wiki/Melvil_Dewey

This practice works well until you have more than one article with the same name, at which point you need to add something to disambiguate the term:

http://en.wikipedia.org/wiki/Pluto_(mythology)

http://en.wikipedia.org/wiki/Pluto_(Disney)

Disambiguation is one of the main functions of name authority control in libraries. The LC Subject Heading file gives each of these two Plutos a different name and a different identifier:

Pluto (Greek deity) http://id.loc.gov/authorities/sh85103581

Pluto (Fictitious character) http://id.loc.gov/authorities/sh96010495

Disambiguation becomes more difficult and less meaningful as the number of items with the same name increases. For names of persons, there are often very many instances of the same name. The library name authority file, where possible, disambiguates with dates of birth and death. This, too, becomes less useful over time.—for instance, between these two:

Fitzgerald, Michael, 1955

Fitzgerald, Michael, 1955 June 11

Only family and dear friends will have the information necessary to pick out the person they are seeking in the library catalog. Yet, because these two individuals are separately identified, they are different.

Internet Engineering Task Force
www.ietf.org

The subjects or names may confuse human readers, but once they are assigned identifiers, machines will have no problem knowing the difference. In this case, Pluto (Greek deity) is not a display form of the name since LCSH uses instead "Hades (Greek deity)" with "Pluto (Greek Deity)" as a cross reference. Both, however, are identified with http://id.loc.gov/authorities/sh85103581 and will be considered the same subject when used in a Semantic Web context. In the same way, the various persons named Michael Fitzgerald will each be given a unique identifier that will make them clearly distinguished for any machine processes.

URIs and URLs

The general wisdom among developers of the Semantic Web functionality is that the best identifiers are URIs (Uniform Resource Identifiers), and the best URIs are URLs (Uniform Resource Locators). Because URLs are URIs (but with the specific purpose of providing a Web location for something), URLs can be used as identifiers as well as locations. Among the advantages of using URLs is that they can easily be used to return information about the thing being identified, as using the HTTP (Hypertext Transfer Protocol) directs browsers and other programs to retrieve documents on the Web. In the case of an identifier, what you might retrieve is a description of what is being identified. The machine functions will work well with a string of characters that have little or no meaning to a human, yet there can also be human-friendly data attached to the identifier, and it can be found by following the identifier to its Web location.

An example is a Semantic Web language called Friend of a Friend (FOAF). This language allows you to describe people, particularly in a social networking environment. FOAF has fields for the common personal elements used in social networking sites like name, sex, birthday, and e-mail address. An identifier for a person could return this FOAF information in a display so that human users could see information that means more to them than an identifier. An example from the FOAF documentation shows a person's name and his work home page address:

```
<foaf:Person>

    <foaf:name>Dan Brickley</foaf:name>

    <foaf:workplaceHomepage
    rdf:resource="http://www.w3.org/"/>

</foaf:Person>
```

This information could be located at a URL that is used to identify Dan Brickley as a member of the W3C (the World Wide Web Consortium), for example: http://w3c.org/people/dbrickley. Whenever one refers to Dan Brickley in Semantic Web data, one could use this identifier.

An example from the library world is the online version of the Library of Congress Subject Headings that has been made available by the Library in linked data format. There is a separate identifier for each entry in the subject authority file, about 350,000 total. Because the identifier is also a URL, the Library has placed information about the subject heading at that location and can display it in formats for human readers or for programs. When a machine process requests the data, it is returned in one of several possible formats, depending on what was specified in the request. Here is a fragment from the entry for the subject heading "Semantic Web" as it would be returned to the requester in a format called RDF/XML:

```
<rdf:Description rdf:about="http://id.loc.gov/
    authorities/sh2002000569#concept">

    <rdf:type rdf:resource="http://www.
    w3.org/2004/02/skos/core#Concept"/>

<skos:broader rdf:resource="http://id.loc.gov/
    authorities/sh2004000479#concept"/>

<skos:prefLabel xml:lang="en">Semantic Web</
    skos:prefLabel>

</rdf:Description>
```

Obviously this is not human-friendly, but the full record that is returned in this format can also be displayed to a human, using the same underlying data, as shown in figure 14.

The ability to return information based on the identifier is one way to extend the Semantic Web, both for machine processing and for the human user. A computer program can use some of the data provided in machine-readable form to make additional connections. For example, the alternate forms of terms in LCSH or the broader and narrower terms can extend a vocabulary search. The e-mail address in a FOAF record could allow an application to offer the option to send an e-mail to the person who is identified. In the end, though, it is people who design and write the programs that are used by computers, and that human understanding is key to the development of information resources. The tool that does the heavy lifting, the computer, is stupidly inanimate.

Of course, it is not reasonable to assume a single system of identifiers for everything on the Web. Undoubtedly, different communities will assign identifiers of their own, some overlapping with those of another community. "Switching stations" will be needed that gather identifiers that are equivalent or nearly so. An example of this is the Virtual International

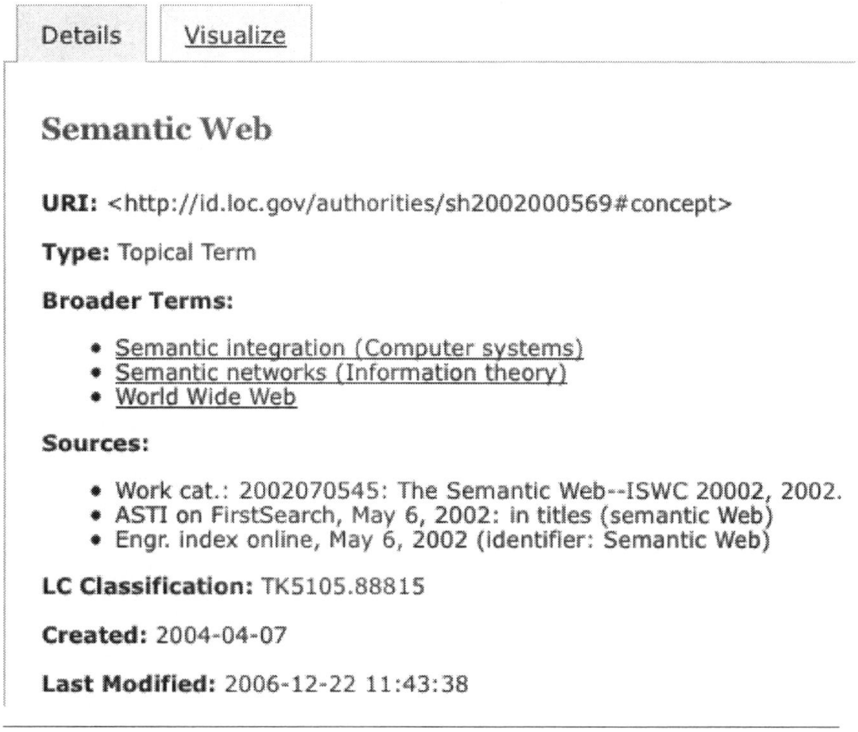

Details	Visualize

Semantic Web

URI: <http://id.loc.gov/authorities/sh2002000569#concept>

Type: Topical Term

Broader Terms:

- Semantic integration (Computer systems)
- Semantic networks (Information theory)
- World Wide Web

Sources:

- Work cat.: 2002070545: The Semantic Web--ISWC 20002, 2002.
- ASTI on FirstSearch, May 6, 2002: in titles (semantic Web)
- Engr. index online, May 6, 2002 (identifier: Semantic Web)

LC Classification: TK5105.88815

Created: 2004-04-07

Last Modified: 2006-12-22 11:43:38

Figure 14
Catalog search for "Semantic Web"

Authority File under development. This file registers equivalent forms of the same name as used by different national libraries. Each library can assign its own identifier, and through the VIAF it will be possible to learn that one library's *Tolstoy, Aleksey Konstantinovich, graf, 1817–1875* is another library's ТОЛСТОЙ, АЛЕКСЕЙ КОНСТАНТИНОВИЧ, ГРАФ, *1817–1875*. They both are identified, however, with http://viaf.org/viaf/20473541.

How Identifiers and Relationships Make the Web Semantic

So far we've seen what identifiers are, but how do they create a Semantic Web? In its simplest form, identifiers allow a computer to act on the elements of Semantic Web statements without understanding their human meaning. For example, suppose you have two things (a circle and a box), and a relationship (arrow), as shown in figure 15. Then you can ask the question shown in figure 16.

An automated system can answer with *Circle* without in any way knowing what any of this means. This doesn't seem to be much, but if *Circle* represents "Herman Melville" and *Box* represents "*Moby Dick, or The Whale*," and the arrow represents the relationship "is author of," then the question can be translated to human language as "Who wrote *Moby Dick, or The Whale*"? And the system can provide the answer: Herman Melville (figure 17).

You can also ask, "Who wrote *Moby Dick*?" and get the answer "Herman Melville." With more statements, you can get more than one answer.

Now you can ask, "What books did Herman Melville write?" and get back a list of two, as shown in figure 18.

Because the Semantic Web would be operating on identifiers, the correct (but much more awkward) original statement would be:

<identifier for Herman Melville> <identifier for "is author of"> <identifier for "Moby Dick or The Whale">

In actual code it could be something like this, using the LC Name Authorities identifier for Melville, the RDVocab property for the author role, and the WorldCat identifier for the book:

<http://id.loc.gov/authorities/n79006936> <http://rdvocab.info/roles/author> <http://www.worldcat.org/oclc/25788271>

As more information is added to the Semantic Web, a greater variety of questions can be answered. The statements create a web of information that can answer questions like "What other books were published by the same publisher in the same year as this edition of *Moby Dick*?" as shown in figure 19.

The extraction of meaningful information from the web of data requires a method to query the Web in a structured way. The standard for querying databases is a language known as Structured Query Language (SQL). The linked data community has developed a query language, called SPARQL (pronounced "sparkle"), that operates similarly on the Semantic Web. SPARQL is relatively new, and the tools available for using it are suitable primarily for knowledgeable developers. However, we can

Figure 17
Circle and box with values answering one query

Figure 15
Circle → Box.

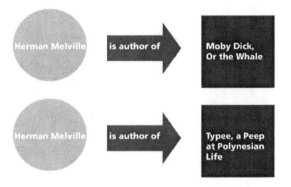

Figure 18
Circle and box with values answering two queries

Figure 16
? → Box.

Understanding the Semantic Web: Bibliographic Data and Metadata **Karen Coyle**

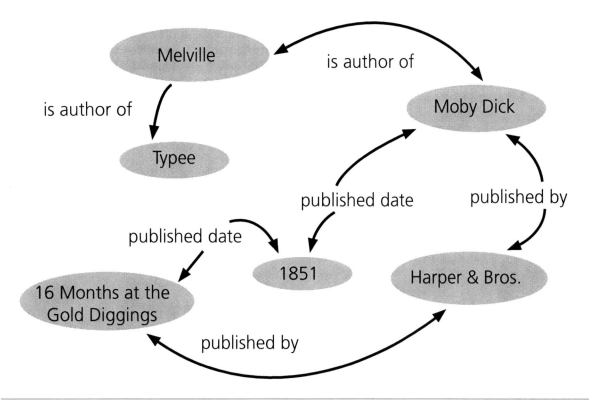

Figure 19
As more data is added to the semantic web, a greater variety of questions can be answered.

expect that as the Semantic Web progresses, there will be interfaces that allow more of us to experiment with querying the Semantic Web and the great variety of data that is in the linked data cloud.

Key Characteristics of the Semantic Web

There are specific characteristics of the Semantic Web that make it particularly appropriate for the broad reach of information and the dynamic nature of information today. First, the Semantic Web is **dynamic**. Unlike the linking that takes place in database management systems, where links have to be created internally between items, linking on the Web is dynamic and automatic. Think of what happens when you add a hyperlink to a document: the mere existence of the HTTP address in the link creates the connection between the current document and what it links to, and that link is active immediately. With the Semantic Web, data added to the Web in Semantic Web format will be able to link and be accessed immediately without any further programming. The disadvantage to the dynamic nature of the Web and the Semantic Web is that nothing stays the same for very long. Searches done at one time will turn up different results when done again later if new resources and new information have been added to the Semantic Web.

The Web is a **global** information resource, although each user tends to see only a particular slice that responds to her area of interest. While most online documents will be seen by only a small percentage of Internet users, there is no way to predict who will make use of the online data or how they will use it. We have to assume that the context for any online data is the entire Web itself. This is in contrast to data stored in databases, where the data needs to be defined and identified only within the context of that particular database. Even with the sharing of library metadata on a large scale, the context for the data is assumed to be that of library standards. On the Web, library data will interact with data that was created in other contexts by nonlibrarians and for other purposes. The global nature of the Web means that there are an untold number of possible uses of the data, but also a great variety in the data sources. A less controlled environment has disadvantages, such as unevenness in the quality of resources. However, by structuring metadata in a way that it can be used on the global Internet, it can be used anywhere on the Web without ambiguity.

An advantage of the networked environment for metadata is its **extensibility**. New data and data types can be added at any time. Mashups, or the recombination of data from different sources, actually create new information, even if only temporarily as the outcome of a search over multiple sources. This has an effect on the standards process, of course. Changes and additions do not have to be pre-announced for the Web to continue working as it does. The Web itself becomes the standard communication platform, providing notification of changes and downloadable versions of new and proposed elements and values. Changes can proliferate quickly throughout the community using the data.

A key element of the Semantic Web is that there are meaningful **relationships** between things. We don't just link John and Mary, we are able to say what that link means. It could be that John is the son of Mary, or Mary the manager of John. These are very different statements, but on the Web today you cannot make this distinction with hyperlinks. It is this addition of relationships to the hyperlinking of the Web that can transform the Web from what it is today to a richer, more meaningful information environment.

Linked (Open) Data

The Semantic Web as introduced by Tim Berners-Lee is a linked web of information encoded in documents throughout the web. Achievement of this vision is still over the visible horizon. In practice, however, there is a growing community of people and organizations who have metadata available to them that they have structured using Semantic Web rules. These disparate sets of data can be combined into a base of actionable data. These sets of data are being referred to as "linked data," and the Linked Data Cloud is an open and informal representation of compatible data available over the Internet. New linked data is being added to the cloud daily. Each new resource that is added to the Web in this format increases the number of data connections that are possible between

Linked Data Cloud
http://linkeddata.org

existing data sets.

Many of the early participants in linked data are institutions with already existing scientific data sets. Linking allows data from PubMed records, for example, to link to scientific databases like the Protein Databank, the Human Gene Nomenclature Database, and Chemical Entities of Biological Interest database. There are also some general purpose data sets available, such as geographic names, U.S. Census data, and the wealth of names and facts from Wikipedia. Helping to bring these sets of data together is a particular data set called Dbpedia. The core of Dbpedia is an extraction of coded data from Wikipedia, with related links added from a variety of linked data sources on the open Web. A few of the items of interest in the lengthy set of data about Herman Melville in Dbpedia include

the date and place of his birth and death, the various subject headings and genres that have been assigned to his works, writers who influenced him and those he influenced.[10] This information displays in Dbpedia in a rather unfriendly, pseudo-code form, but the data is intended primarily to be used for linking by programs taking advantage of Semantic Web capabilities. Here is an excerpt from the Dbpedia page on Herman Melville:

dbpedia-owl:Person/birthDate

1819-08-01 (xsd:date)

dbpedia-owl:Person/birthPlace

dbpedia:New_York_City

dbpedia:United_States

dbpedia:New_York

dbpedia-owl:Person/deathDate

1891-09-28 (xsd:date)

dbpedia-owl:Person/deathPlace

dbpedia:New_York_City

dbpedia:United_States

dbpedia:New_York

It is somewhat difficult to explain what you can do with linked open data because the answer is just about anything. Where data can be combined on any data element, you can do data mining in the linked open data space in the same way that you would in a database. A geographic name in a text could be linked to a geographic name in a database that returns longitude and latitude, or one that links to historical information, images, and photographs, or even genealogy data. In our Herman Melville case, data of this nature could be used to gather a list of authors born in a particular era and a particular place. Mining of this data is available openly to anyone on the Web, and there is no way to predict the uses that might be discovered.

Imagine, therefore, what possibilities there would be if all of the bibliographic data from all of the library catalogs of the world were added to the mix. We've said that the value of linked data increases with every node that joins the linked data space. This is also true with library data as linked data. Data from a single library will add many interesting data points from new cataloged resources, but as each library's data is added, new kinds

WorldCat Identities
http://orlabs.oclc.org/Identities

Library Technology Reports   www.alatechsource.org   January 2010

of information can be extracted. Not only will more libraries add new titles, the repeated information from the holdings of many libraries can be useful. The value of library holdings is evident in the WorldCat Identities project produced by the OCLC Research Division. While information about a single book can tell you who the author is, and where and when it was published, information about how many libraries hold a book can add qualitative information, like which are the most frequently held books by or about a person. Linked open data has the potential to foster the discovery of new information as users find interesting ways to combine it.

To understand how linked data becomes information we can look again at our sentence about Herman Melville and *Moby Dick*. Data provided in linked data form in Dbpedia gives useful dates, links to works by the author, and more. Library data, both from WorldCat Identities and library catalog records, contains information that could fill in some gaps in the current linked data view of this work. Library data cannot participate, however, until that catalog is made available in the

Dbpedia
http://dbpedia.org

linked data format.

What can libraries offer that no other community can? First, libraries have vast holdings of published and unpublished materials that are not currently represented on the Web. Next, they have metadata for most of those materials. The metadata includes controlled forms of personal and corporate names, physical description, topical headings, and classification assignments. This data could interact with almost any information on the Web, since libraries cover the full range of human endeavor in their holdings.

The entry of library data into the linked data cloud is not a replacement for library catalogs. Indeed, the functions related to library management like inventory control, acquisitions, and materials handling will continue to be part of the institutional database used by libraries. What is gained from the transformation of library data to linked data is an entry into a larger information universe that reaches users on the Web and can be exploited in combination with any other data that is found there. The Semantic Web is a logical extension of the information services provided to library users and is one that could greatly expand the number and range of persons who benefit from the library.

The movement of library data into the linked data cloud is not as far off as it might seem. Like the scientific databases, the metadata already exists and is in a data format. Some transformation of the data to a format compatible with the Semantic Web will be necessary, but the encoding that has already been done (mainly in the MARC format) and the degree of vocabulary control that exists facilitate the transformation. It truly is a matter of transformation, at least in a first step. After that, the only limits are those of the imagination of information seekers all over the globe.

Notes

1. *On the Record: Report of the Library of Congress Working Group on the Future of Bibliographic Control* (Washington, DC: Library of Congress, Jan. 9, 2008), 26, www.loc.gov/bibliographic-future/news/lcwg-ontherecord-jan08-final.pdf (accessed Nov. 17, 2009).
2. Ibid, 24; Roy Tennant, "MARC Must Die," *Library Journal*, Oct. 15, 2002, www.libraryjournal.com/article/CA250046.html (accessed Nov. 17, 2009).
3. Tim Berners-Lee, "Information Management, a Proposal," March 1989, www.w3.org/History/1989/proposal.html (accessed Nov. 17, 2009); Vannevar Bush, "As We May Think," *The Atlantic*, July 1945, www.theatlantic.com/doc/194507/bush (accessed Nov. 17, 2009).
4. Tim Berners-Lee, James Hendler, and Ora Lassila, "The Semantic Web," *Scientific American*, May 2001, 34–43.
5. Bruce Sterling, *The Hacker Crackdown: Law and Disorder on the Electronic Frontier* (New York: Bantam Books, 1992), 31.
6. International Organization for Standardization, "Numeric Representations of Dates and Time," ISO website, FAQ pages, www.iso.org/iso/date_and_time_format (accessed Nov. 17, 2009).
7. Tim Berners-Lee, "Universal Resource Identifiers: Axioms of Web Architecture," World Wide Web Consortium website, Dec. 19, 1996, www.w3.org/DesignIssues/Axioms.html (accessed Nov. 17, 2009).
8. Dublin Core Metadata Initiative, "DCMI Metadata Terms," Jan. 14, 2008, http://dublincore.org/documents/dcmi-terms (accessed Nov. 17, 2009).
9. J. Hakala and H. Walravens, "Using International Standard Book Numbers as Uniform Resource Names," Internet Engineering Task Force website, Oct. 2001, www.ietf.org/rfc/rfc3187.txt (accessed Nov. 17, 2009).
10. "About Herman Melville," Dbpedia, http://dbpedia.org/page/Herman_Melville (accessed Nov. 17, 2009).

Resources

Metadata

Caplan, Priscilla. *Metadata Fundamentals for All Librarians*. Chicago: American Library Association, 2003.

A basic introduction to metadata concepts with an emphasis on metadata used in the cultural heritage and learning communities. The text covers the Text Encoding Initiative (TEI), Dublin Core, Encoded Archival Description (EAD), and government and geospatial metadata. In addition, it addresses categories of metadata beyond resource description, such as administrative and rights metadata.

Hillmann, Diane, and Elaine Westbrooks, eds. *Metadata in Practice*. Chicago: American Library Association, 2004.

The sixteen essays in this book cover a wide range of metadata projects. The emphasis is on the decisions that go into successful metadata development. The editors cite these primary lessons: change happens in this area too rapidly for one to wait for concrete standards to emerge before embarking on metadata development; and it is vital to document any variance from standards so that others can understand and potentially share metadata.

Semantic Web

Berners-Lee, Tim, James Hendler, and Ora Lassila. "The Semantic Web." *Scientific American Magazine*, May 2001. Available for purchase at www.sciam.com/article.cfm?id=the-semantic-web (accessed Nov. 19, 2009).

The Semantic Web was introduced to the general public in this *Scientific American* article by Tim Berners-Lee and colleagues.

World Wide Web Consortium. W3C Semantic Web Activity. www.w3.org/2001/sw.

The development of standards for the Semantic Web is based in the World Wide Web Consortium. The project includes numerous individual standards, such as the Resource Description Framework (RDF), Simple Knowledge Organization System (SKOS), and the Web Ontology Language (OWL). Few of the standards documents are suitable for novices in the area. A possible starting point is "RDF Primer" (www.w3.org/TR/rdf-primer) by Miller and Manola.

Catalogs and Cataloging

Calhoun, Karen. *The Changing Nature of the Catalog and Its Integration with Other Discovery Tools.* Washington, DC: Library of Congress, March 17, 2006. www.loc.gov/catdir/calhoun-report-final.pdf (accessed Nov. 19, 2009).

This analysis of the decline of library catalogs in the increasingly Web-based world was highly disruptive when issued, but also opened the door to new thinking about catalogs, cataloging, and the future. Calhoun used structured interviews with leaders in the library field to surface key issues facing libraries in these times. This report is valuable for its methodology as well as its conclusions. Includes a significant bibliography on the topic.

On the Record: Report of The Library of Congress Working Group on the Future of Bibliographic Control. Washington, DC: Library of Congress, January 9, 2008. www.loc.gov/bibliographic-future/news/lcwg-ontherecord-jan08-final.pdf.

Convened by the Library of Congress, the Working Group considered bibliographic control in general and investigated issues relating to management of library data and catalogs as well as the current technology context. As the Library pursues recommendations from the report, these are presented on the Working Group website: www.loc.gov/bibliographic-future.

Tillett, Barbara. Resource *Description and Access: Background/Overview* (webcast). Washington, DC: Library of Congress, May 14, 2008, www.loc.gov/today/cyberlc/feature_wdesc.php?rec=4320 (accessed Nov. 19, 2009).

Tillett, Barbara. *Cataloging Principles and RDA: Resource Description and Access* (webcast). Washington, DC: Library of Congress, June 10, 2008, www.loc.gov/today/cyberlc/feature_wdesc.php?rec=4327 (accessed Nov. 19, 2009).

In these two webcasts, Barbara Tillett introduces RDA (Resource Description and Access), the next-generation cataloging code designed for the digital environment. The first presentation covers the general principles that guided the creation of RDA and gives information on the structure of new code. It also places RDA in its historical context in relation to prior cataloging codes. The second webcast talks about the International Cataloging Principles and emphasizes the role of such principles in creating successful catalogs.

Library Technology Reports Respond to Your Library's Digital Dilemmas

Eight times per year, *Library Technology Reports* (LTR) provides library professionals with insightful elucidation, covering the technology and technological issues the library world grapples with on a daily basis in the information age.

Library Technology Reports 2010, Vol. 46	
January 46:1	**"Understanding the Semantic Web: Bibliographic data and Metadata"** by Karen Coyle, Digital Library Consultant
February/ March 46:2	**"RDA Vocabularies for a 21st-Century Data Environment"** by Karen Coyle, Digital Library Consultant
April 46:3	**"Gadgets & Gizmos: Personal Electronics at your Library"** by Jason Griffey, Head of Library Information Technology, University of Tennessee at Chattanooga
May/June 46:4	**"Object Re-Use and Exchange (OAI-ORE)"** by Mike Witt, Interdisciplinary Research Librarian & Assistant Professor of Library Science, Purdue University Libraries
July 46:5	**"Web-Based Voice and Video: Investigating Library Applications and Challenges"** by Char Booth, E-Learning Librarian, University of California, Berkeley
August/ September 46:6	**"Understanding Electronic Resources Usage: a Review of the State of the Art"** by Jill E. Grogg, E-Resources Librarian, University of Alabama Libraries, and Rachel Fleming-May, Assistant Professor, School of Information Sciences at the University of Tennessee
October 46:7	**"Open URL"** by Cindi Trainor, Coordinator for Library Technology & Data Services at Eastern Kentucky University, and Jason Price, E-resource Package Analyst, Statewide California Electronic Library Consortium
November/ December 46:8	**"Privacy and Freedom of Information in 21st Century Libraries"** by the ALA Office of Information Freedom, Chicago, IL

ALA TechSource

www.alatechsource.org

ALA TechSource, a unit of the publishing department of the American Library Association

LaVergne, TN USA
11 November 2010

204404LV00002B/2/P

9 780838 958070